OUR
HANDS
HOLD
VIOLENCE

THE NATIONAL POETRY SERIES

The National Poetry Series was established in 1978 to ensure
the publication of five collections of poetry annually through
five participating publishers. The series is funded annually by the
Academy of American Poets/Amazon Literary Partnership, William
Geoffrey Beattie, the Gettinger Family Foundation, Bruce Gibney, the
Tabitha and Stephen King Foundation, Anna and Olafur Olafsson,
Penguin Random House, the Poetry Foundation, the Gil Schwartz
Foundation, and the National Poetry Series Board of Directors.

THE NATIONAL POETRY SERIES
WINNERS OF THE 2024 OPEN COMPETITION

82nd Division by D. M. Aderibigbe
Chosen by Colin Channer for Akashic Books

Blue Loop by AJ White
Chosen by Chelsea Dingman for University of Georgia Press

Games for Children by Keith Wilson
Chosen by Rosalie Moffett for Milkweed Editions

Shade Is a Place by MaKshya Tolbert
Chosen by Maggie Millner for Penguin

Our Hands Hold Violence by Kieron Walquist
Chosen by Brenda Hillman for Beacon Press

OUR
HANDS
HOLD
VIOLENCE

POEMS

KIERON WALQUIST

WITH A FOREWORD BY
BRENDA HILLMAN

BEACON PRESS, BOSTON

BEACON PRESS
Boston, Massachusetts
www.beacon.org

Beacon Press books
are published under the auspices of
the Unitarian Universalist Association of Congregations.

28 27 26 25   8 7 6 5 4 3 2 1

This book is printed on acid-free paper that meets the uncoated paper
ANSI/NISO specifications for permanence as revised in 1992.

Text design and composition by Kim Arney

*Library of Congress Cataloging-in-Publication
Data is available for this title.*
ISBN: 978-0-8070-2125-5; e-book: 978-0-8070-2126-2

The authorized representative in the EU for product safety and
compliance is Easy Access System Europe 16879218, Mustamäe tee 50,
10621 Tallinn, Estonia: http://beacon.org/eu-contact.

To my family, blood + other
+ to Missouri.

SKELETON

FOREWORD

Kieron Walquist has written a gorgeous, moving book. I was immediately drawn to these poems because they bear frequent rereading, are musically and formally various, mix tonalities of the vernacular and the slightly oracular, have subtle and original takes on experience, and have oblique and fresh ideas about how to recast personal events in a world of homophobia and bias. The lines and the structures yield new elements together. Walquist's book is a coming out story that is also a survival story and a story of adaptation; it interrogates images of dysfunctional masculinity in the heart of American culture, explores memories of childhood that includes unpredictable violence and paradoxical truths. It is also a story of neighborhoods and communities that adapt, or fail to, in light of the variety of people found there. The poet's vivid vocabulary deploys both literary and technical references, including descriptions of machinery, tools, and workplaces of rural life—literal and metaphorical. This poet's writing can be at times tender, at times terrifying and ominous. The visual hybrid elements engage the eye and the brain with fast shifts. The poet has a keen sense of how to use ironic detail, describing neighborhoods that degrade by accretion, that must accommodate themselves to toxic elements. We are reminded that beauty, the capacity for self-understanding, and the insistence on a conscious life of language, love, and imagination are stronger than violence.

—BRENDA HILLMAN
2024

HERE

Hometown

Hartsburg, Missouri

A coyote cry that tears through sleep
in the country-dark. The bleats
+ bells from goats heavy with milk,
the creek that overflows + leaves
crawdads + catfish breathless
in backyards. The ditch
where folks toss their trash:
tires, television sets, a Maytag
washer. A boy abusing
Sudafed. A three-legged bluetick
never let off its chain. The rumor
of a cougar deep in the hills,
a caved-in septic tank that can drop
you, drown you. A cathedral of cedars,
the tumble-down barn with warped
wood, the abandoned car rusted
+ broken into by musk thistle.
The dynamite blast from the quarry
that rattles windows, the fog flung
over the valley like a mortuary sheet.

Past + Present Billboards Outside Jefferson City, Missouri

March 30th, 2007—The molestation case against Jefferson City funeral director and businessman Reid Millard has been dismissed. Less than a week before his trial was scheduled to begin, Cole County Prosecutor Mark Richardson has formerly withdrawn the criminal complaint.

In 2005, former prosecutor Bill Tackett charged Millard with sodomy, based on the boy's story that he was fondled by Millard while staying at his home, and on DNA evidence collected there.

—KRCG 13

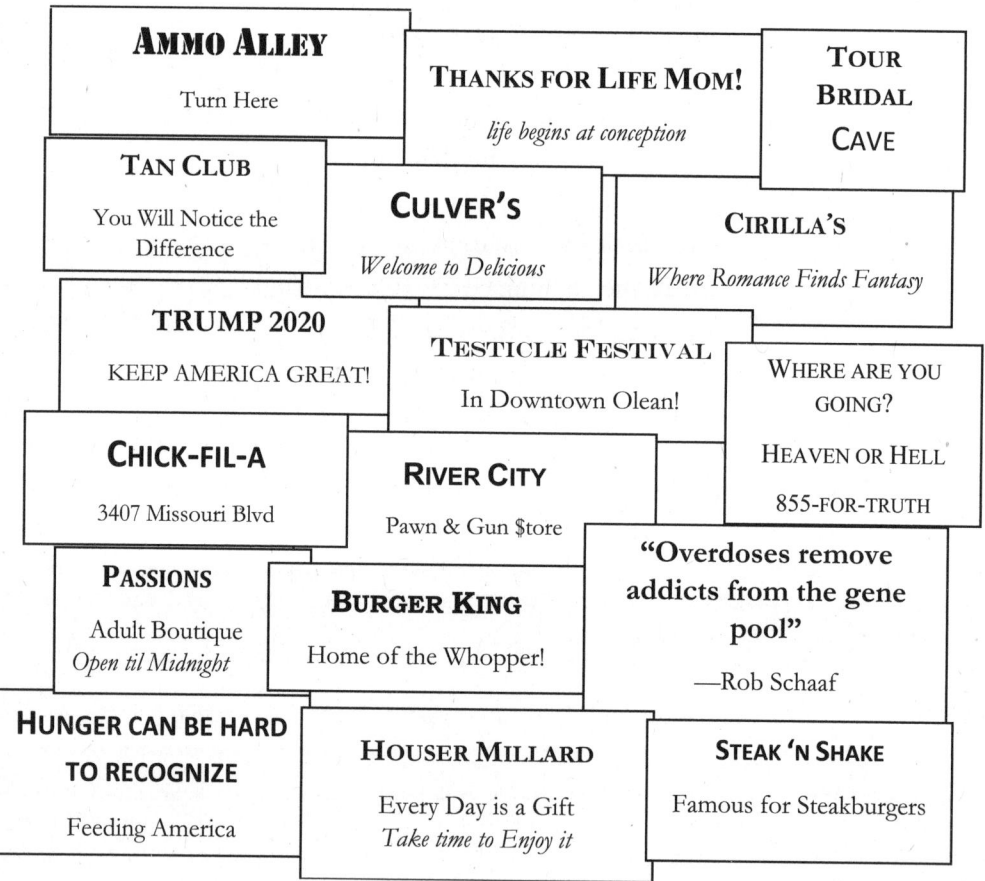

Want

The blue + gray-mucked dumpster
at Moser's groceries is the only grave
mother says she'll put us in.
We're scavenger birds
for her pride—taking what's free,
what's there, because we're told
it's good before it's all-the-way
gone. My sisters spoil raspberry-pink,
ashamed—look around
while I'm made to dig in
old cardboard + plastic bags.
I offer up rye bread. Oranges.
A head of lettuce. Button
mushrooms. Rot is a crayon box
of colors: gray white yellow
green blue brown black very
black. Rot is syrup-wet, soft,
whiskery—an inside-turned-out
smell. *What's that
you're holding?* mother asks.
Not want, but food! + she's right—
this cantaloupe, split open
+ soured, is not want.

Halloween

always homemade + never a homerun.
One year, I was a chocolate chip cookie
fashioned from a greasy Pizza Hut box,
polka-dots circled on with a dry-dead
Sharpie. My straps were green + leftover
Easter ribbon, my dumb seven-year-old
slogan: *trick or treat—don't eat me!*

+ no one got it.

Door after door, adults
with bowls of Milk Duds + Skittles
would stare me down, while I held out
my sleep-slobbered pillowcase + peeked
inside their clean, quiet houses.
Even the crackheads in the duplexes
up the road [we were told not to go,
but they had king-size candy]
stopped + said, *What the hell are you
supposed to be?*

I never had an answer.

Hillbilly Swimming Pool

To be in those Aprils again
    when the red truck
        parked on a hill
+ it rained enough,
    so we shoved kitchen towels
        down the tailgate crack to keep
the hurricane from draining;
    picked leaves + sticks from the flood
        + waded in, sat crisscross-applesauce,
our bony backs against questionable metal,
    + shouted at father to *Drive as fast as you can!*—
        how he did, then; took turns like a madman,
pumped the brakes way too often,
    the water a bathtub-wash
        over us. We screamed + shivered,
sliced open
    with such incredible joy.

RollerCoaster Tycoon® + the Tyrant I Was

Axed all the trees + ignored AI comments on
Beauty. Built one bathroom, far away, +
Charged $5 to use it. Colored cotton candy a
Dirty-snow. Drove the janitors to death
Emptying trash + erasing pixelated vomit.
Fired them in front of the Ferris Wheel.
Gave up on the grass + let it jungle, outlawed
Hotdog stands + Helicopter Hats. Forced
Ice cream cones out of innocent hands by
Jolting people into the jewelry-blue sky, a
Kind of temporary kidnapping, only to
Let them drop above the Log Flume + drown.
Milked the line to the Merry-Go-Round until
No one wanted to navigate it + all walked
Out. Operated during simulated storms,
Paused the game + time itself to suspend panic.
Queued mascots to dance in the queasy-heat.
Ran rollercoasters nonstop—sent riders
Screaming along twisted steel that kicked sparks,
Twice exploded, + tanked the park's ratings.
Undid pavement + left patrons lost on the
Very corners of the virtual landscape.
Withheld water fountains + wasted hours.
X-rayed thoughts but X-ed out complaints
Yapping on about prices, safety, the yuck drying.
Zeroed in on every name + *zing*—changed it to mine.

Happy Meal® | Monopoly

OREO MCFLURRY OR
PRAY FOR NAVY ACRES,
$1 MILLION, + FORGET
10PC NUGGETS FLY-
BUBBLING OUT], + WE
WAITING FOR MIRACLES

EXP 04/01/09
RULES APPLY
B44RQL89

MED. FRY, WE PEEL +
REAL ESTATE WORTH
TO EAT OR DRINK [OUR
BOMBED, OUR SPRITE
FORGET OUR YOUTH,
ON TINY SLIPS OF PAPER

EXP 04/01/09
RULES APPLY
J3X9BRN9

Tractor Implements: A Manual

The tiller:
- stays behind the shed, in a gush of goldenrod,
  + sulks.
- takes us all day to hitch it right. After, we're wrung out
  by July's heat—the soap-sting of sweat
  in our eyes.
- breaks the granite ground. A killing ground,
  where shards of arrowheads glint—
  intense as an ice rink.
- is for you, so you can plant
  those tomatoes
  before it rains.

The chipper shredder:
- weighs more than 500lbs. A mammoth
  machine—death wish on a hill.
- will confetti cedar, branches bare
  or loud with blue
  juniper.
- has backfired, hacked smoke from sap,
  shaken my arm so hard I went numb—
  meat of muscle about to fall
  from bone.
- is for you, so you can have
  a bed of mulch
  for your daylilies.

The brush hog:
- runs all summer long. Most days, we wear the diseased-
  look of grease on our hands, underneath
  fingernails.
- disrupts the itchy sleep of grasshoppers, scaring
  them airborne—a holy plague
  upon a hushed property.

    · has decapitated a rabbit before. Our cat resurrected
      its soft head on the front porch—
      flesh + blood
      all bubblegum.
    · is for you, so you can breathe
      in the air
      without sneezing.

The paving blade:
    · tears itself in the sun, steel
      now a terracotta color.
    · goes on the Kubota after a storm, where the wash
      cuts canyons from our driveway—
      down to open veins
      of clay.
    · rubs against the gravel, striking
      thunder.
    · is for you, mother, so you can come home
      safe. + we can love
      until love
      isn't a chore.

O Iron Giant: Establishing Shot

Space	:	a gold pan, sluicing itself.
Earth	:	blue streak, fossil of before + now + after, streaked blue.
Our birth	:	comet-crash.
The night	:	scarred with rain + lightning like a welding torch.
The town	:	More pumpkins than people.
Our mother	:	████████████
Our father	:	absent
Us	:	machine/man, water-tower-tall. Parts fair + impaired.
The man who finds us	:	open-mouthed.

Always

Lake of the Ozarks, Missouri

Ten years old in a drug-dirty
trailer home, locked

in the bathroom [tub
+ toilet scummed in calcium]

trying to put K-mart trunks over
my wasp waist + I don't want to,

but I walk down a nail-toothed dock
that's decorated with spiders the size

of Christmas lights + Styrofoam coolers
browned by carp in spit-warm water

+ I don't want him to, but my father pulls
a moldy lifejacket over my bone-white

chest + I don't want to—because *it
doesn't fit*—but he puts me

on a jet ski + we leave the cove
[its summer cabins + party inflatables]

+ I don't want to, but we rip + roar
on that blue-green surface + roll the jet ski,

tear a hole through + slip into nothingness,
+ when I pop up, puking froth, my father's

gone, just behind the craft, but I believe he's
drowned before I ever made him proud

of me + I will, somehow, always be
ten years old, wet + wounded

hollering *what do I
do what do I do what do I—*

Gorgeous

I'm a buzz cut + braces, scarecrow-skinny, ready for
my friend's pirated P90X video to show me a hunger
worth wearing. Shirts off, we drink protein [which is

a papier-mâché paste] + pump dumbbells to
get ripped in 90 days! In his basement, we give

each other grief—*no, like this*—+ perfect the
form, the rep, by shadowing the TV. His body
brushes mine after we try pushups. It's not what

I was expecting—firm but I could fall into it,
like a mattress. *Sorry,* I say, + hope he knows

our chest bump means nothing. He laughs about it
+ dries off. Rubs at his neck, back. In the mirror, we cannot
help but flex. After, he hands me his towel [wet] to keep.

THERE

XXX

The K-mart men

exist

in the back
by the boots,
too far from the

exit

+ pharmacy
for my mother to

expect

me to wander + get lost
down,

except

I do wander the aisle,
not lost but

excited

by something
I'm somewhat afraid
of—
that men in

XXX

esque pictures are

exquisite,

wholly or just torsos—
full of bravado—
boxers + briefs—
those bodies + poses
I cannot pull off—
how I

exhale

too loudly
before the blond
lifting his tank top,

exposing

belly button—stomach all
exercise

+ canyon-bare—my hands
now on the package,
holding it
up to florescent-light—an

                X-ray

                                that shows myself
                                back to myself,
                                where what was broken
                                was only

                exiled

+ made to feel broken—
heaven is here
if you want it—
+ I take it,

                excuse

                                myself as I move
                                around another shopper.

Remains

Outside Jefferson City, Missouri

I.
The buck carwrecked
now rests + rots on an isle
of bird's-foot trefoil
off Hwy 63. My brother + I
brake [our father's truck
lade for pawn shops]
+ coast over. I pet its coat,
comb my fingers full
with it, while my brother
gets his hacksaw
to harvest its antlers—
its small coatrack.
'Cause he'll rattle the bones
when hunting. 'Cause
we can't leave
any crime scene alone.
The buck is puffy,
glammed by greenbottle
flies, + behind us, slaughter-
red streak-dry
across the asphalt
like ketchup down a t-shirt.
The smell of it churns.
My brother cuts bone
from skull. I try
to hold the body
steady by its front hooves—
two black hearts. I tell
myself to *Get through*.
I look away when I see—
in the copper-cool
of its eye—me.

II.

The prison sits + scares
on a floodplain, a former farm
of corn + soybean that borders
a muddy Missouri riverbank.
Since the flood of '93,
it shrivels for *no more*:
whitewashed + wicker,
blood-orange rebar
worn out-
side its monolith.
My brother + I trespass
past the night's violet.
We're there to see
ghosts, the gas chamber,
the showers spray-
painted in kitschy +
godawful graffiti:
Satan swastikas Cock-
sucker Hannah Is Hot!
We're there to haunt
something other than us.
By cellphone-light,
my brother + I walk along
cells that snowglobe
with dust, likely asbestos—
he blues an abandoned
sleeping bag, + I
no longer want to be here.
You hear that? my brother
says. + holy shit—
I hear it too.

Any Fire

Jefferson City, Missouri

Something in the heat, the heave,
      the huff, séances us from sleep
to stand before it—

the second house on East Ashley
unfolds a red carpet
      out its windows—

shakes a rage + radiance until
      the firemen soak the fabric
darker, heavier, then still—

when they're tired + headed home,
the house now an ink well,
      we'll scrounge the spill—

for useable pots
      + pans, copper wire,
anything worthwhile—

wonder if the house took like McCarty,
fuse box hot-wired to catch white-
      fire by a vengeful ex-lover—

or if it went up like the one on Lincoln,
      left to dissolve by an oven
left on by the owner—

story goes he'd been shooting up stars,
that the woman on McCarty found
      her man with another man—

but does it matter who's
       the fuel + who's
the flame—

we follow devastation,
walk in that house
       when it isn't ours—

+ return from the woods with a scope eye. Which is to say: you shot yourself lived. + Or, more precisely: you kept your eye on the doe beyond the blackberry patch [the sky was the color of lint + the leaves were wet], you crossed her heart with a fine, fuzzy line, + fired, your eye still pressed to the slightly green lens, the rifle's recoil so powerful that it hole-punched your brow bone + the soft skin beneath. [Your right eye would raccoon for Halloween, perfect for a pirate.] Sister, I'm sure the blood was hot + viscous. That it began to swirl like a kaleidoscope. + swirl + swirl + maybe you saw yourself briefly, on the glass, before you closed + wiped at that eye. Maybe you saw yourself there, the very red of yourself maybe you saw

Headless

Hock | hostage | upside-down crucifixion | a modest
meal | woodblock | tomahawk | wet *thwack* | quiet |

blood-rocket | bird like balloon losing air |
feathers | freakshow | feathers | black feathers

Reptile relax | a belt of brass on the brick pile |
threat of teeth | terrible spit | shovel | severance |

copper now coiling | awful afterlife | just hose
of its throat | trash-fire heat | bog fetor | head ready
+ able to bite | fuck you up later

Boy borderless | oil-slick brain | smeary | siren |
on the spectrum | humbled by | no |
humiliated by | lights that lighthouse | no | chainsaw

through | a few touches | itching
the pink chapel   that is my mouth | myself | freakshow |
hands   like feathers | my head   a beehive | *how do I lose*

my head | + *still run* | no | become less animal |
| no | become okay feeling animal

Cauldron

Attic. Bats caught down eave. Frenzy
gone hush in June's   knifing light.
Myself—no oracle.   Provoked quiet
rascals screaming. Torn under velvety
wings Xing. Yowled   zoic.

What Hunts Us Back

November 13th, 2019—A video circulating social media Wednesday suggested a mountain lion was recently spotted near the Menards on Stonecreek Drive. . . . Using life-sized cutouts as confirmation, agents from the Missouri Department of Conservation said the animal seen in the video is not a cougar.

—KRCG 13

What about Twehous, their years of drilling + dynamite?

The acres knocked down for the new Sam's Club?

+ the tracks found on Campbell's farm, bigger than any housecat or coyote?

The calf dragged off pasture?

[Poor limbs pretzeled.]

What about the footage from Randy's trail cam?

[That low slink + shudder of beige. Those great green eyes.]

The claw marks on Jackie's quarter horse, Fancy?

[How the scratch was the size of a baseball glove + just as dark.]

What about 2008, the lion bulldozed near Fulton, curling fender with fur?

[Its terrifying majesty the first thing you see at the Runge Center.]

+ the flyers, all those little dogs, tacked on Moser's bulletin board?

Why do the men, at Hwy 63 Quarry, carry pistols when entering the mines?

February 9th, when something rode the wind other than fog?

Or the morning a woman caterwauled + wrapped birdsong inside-out.

What about the doe discovered up in a walnut tree, its carcass a chandelier?

The night when the neighborhood dogs wouldn't stop barking.

Wash

You blueprint a body | cookie-cut an acre | pour concrete |
raise lumber | but forget about winter | our labor in limbo | the wind a bullet |
the half-built a whole lot of holes | target paper|
yes | I'm Sunday-slow | mix Phillips + hex
screwdrivers | am no help | am obscene + obnoxious | my Walkman
loud | like a pinball machine | I stim | silly-shake | shadowbox | across
plywood + drywall scraps | kick up sawdust | power cords
+ yes | you're right | I'm lost |
in my own world |
may never learn | you knock a door off | its hinges | saddle it
to two sawhorses | palm the DeWalt sander | mustard-yellow |
y'know | my world
includes you | of course it does | you're there | father | with me |
hey look | here's you plugging in the sander | it pulls power | flickers the light
| the whirr
when you sand | cyclone | kick up sawdust |
hey listen | once you're done we can hear Van Halen |
on KCMQ | Classic Rock | our radio paint-splattered | + precarious |
on an overturned bucket | here we varnish || dip the sleeve of an old t-shirt
into the stain |
walnut | dark as Folger's coffee |
Jesus Christ | the fumes | the force | burrowing a hole
in the head | listen | we're laughing | washing the woodgrain |
its curlicues | we count the lines | the years out loud | leave it to gloss | leave
to wash
at the well | our breath in the cold | sanding | cyclones |
I'm here | right here | learning | you teach me |
to get varnish off your hands | you must wash them |
in gasoline

FEARFEST

Columbia, Missouri

Rather unimpressed by the monsters
that're supposed to be scary:

the hick with a toothless
chainsaw + Budweiser-belly;

the freaky girl + her ragdoll
probably bought at a yard sale.

That hoss hollering about carving
me to pieces? A gas station attendant

at Casey's, the one who chaws
sunflower seeds + spits in a Solo cup.

That possessed princess
fingering her doll's eye socket?

The niece of that lady who shampoos
dogs with her wedding rings on.

Yet still, in the October chill, I wait
with you for the 20-dollar horror.

We watch young [straight] couples
hold one another in prom pose

+ shuffle slow. Already they're scared:
of the night's potential, of pissing

• 28 •

themselves or using the port-a-potty.
You jab at my side, trying to scare me.

Nothing's scary out here—
just high corn + hormonal teens,

an old farmhouse. I part black plastic
+ descend into someone else's nightmare.

It's tacky + thrown together:
a child's bedroom, a butcher's meat freezer,

a circus tent with clowns gone hoarse
from wicked laughter. It's not scary.

But when a skeleton-man emerges
from nowhere, neon-green +

graveyard-wailing, we all touch—
you have my waist + I bearhug

your side, the actor
gripping our shoulders.

We're not supposed to touch.
Or scream each other's name.

Black Cat

4th of July   charcoaled sky

in throes   throbs   a field of flowers—

white peony   to silver palm pistil   red dahlia

        crackling chrysanthemum—

when the boy pulls   a bottle rocket

from a bouquet   of bombs   held

     by a brown paper bag   + lights it

             it's easy it's   *easy*

the fuse fizzles out   so the boy leans

over   the cola bottle + looks down

on the launch site   it's not a dud

just   slow

the boy breaks his pretty face

    about in two

           poppy petals melting

through   his hands   *I can't see   I can't*

see   + from where I stand   I see

the boy   caught in a corkscrew of smoke—

    sulfur + saltpeter   + savagery—

the glint in his   light blue irises

the receipt   folded neatly   in my back pocket

TOGETHER

Border Collie

Death is familiar on a farm. No, all over. In the shed: fly ribbon blackened + sizzling with wings; the buck hung by its hind hooves from the rafters to drip red + dry; the bobcat we caught in a foot trap + skinned after, its coat [bunched in cockleburs] on a shelf starry with salt. In the field: a pie tin I've mixed poison in to suffocate possums from the inside; the coyote we jacklight then leave to rot like a jack-o-lantern, ribs left for vultures to guitar-pick. Such death. Familiar because I've made it. Always thought I had to: for our livestock, our livelihood, a little peace of mind. But you. You, old dog, should've died like our pet instead of something feral. Slow + in almighty pain. Scared. The night you bled + let loose in our mudroom on a bed gone bare-flat. I should've grabbed the gun sooner + given you rest.

Special K

My nickname in grade school from a boy who
played basketball while I sat on the bench,
rolled up my socks, my sweatband.

Made sense: *Kieron* was weird-in-the-mouth, like a mouth guard.
Wildly specific: the autistic + skinny-fat kid.

Boys are nothing but clever
in their cruelty.

I saw him today, the boy, now a man,
working the register at PAYLESS.
Was their "going-out-of-business" sale.

Do they still call you Special K?
His tone asking: *do you finally get it?*

I took my sneakers, my new basketball shoes.
No. No one ever called me that, but you.

Isobutyl Nitrite

but the house party's
thunderous, an indoor pool,
so I hear, *I used to be alright,*
right? His lips to my ear,
yellow bottle + red bolt held out
like a wildflower. I sniff. A little
like nail polish, a little
like chlorine. It scratches
back. It's my first time.
                My first time at the YMCA pool,
I almost drowned. Ladies rested back
on towels, dried their turquoise
toes. I was pulled out of the water
like a bicycle, by an older boy
who looked like Sunshine
from *Remember the Titans.*
After, I cried
alone in the locker room.
                At the party, we huff + become light-
headed. Cleaned by VCR cleaner. I kiss him
then kiss him harder. He grabs
my blond hair. We're two boys,
mouth to mouth, trying to rescue
each other.
                I couldn't rescue *Remember the Titans*
from our VCR becoming cannibal—
the VHS eaten alive + the reel, all that black
ribbon, gutted out. What was left glittered
like party streamers. It rippled like light
upon a pool.
                I saw everything, though.
Sunshine + Bertier. When Sunshine,
the new kid, comes to football practice
with long, blond hair. When Bertier
says, *Hey fellas, look at that fruitcake!*

When, in a locker room, Sunshine tells Bertier,
You know what I want, + lunges to kiss him.
The fight between them.

    For a month, I'd lie in bed
+ face the cool wall. Repeat to myself, *You*
know what I want, you know—
Only later did I realize
the kiss, the fight, the smile
on Sunshine's face as a tease,
the joke it was meant to be.

    When I was pulled out of the water,
I heard another—*How do you drown a blond?*
You put a scratch + sniff sticker
at the bottom of a pool.

O Iron Giant: Double Exposure

I.

Bless our lead-acid battery heart!
Botched experiment,
box of auto parts.
What could we have done?
Our engineer forged us
freaks by design:
disproportionate in pewter
armor, dented head
with autistic software.
Forget it. Fuck it.
We, peculiar robot, won't run
forever. Will likely rust sooner.
Let's not reboot injury
Let's not short-circuit us.

II.

+ bless the scrapheap, beatnik
artist Dean. *We like Dean!*
The motorcycle-jacket
confidence, that five-o'clock shadow.
Pictures of a tan + tattooed body
that could out-blush the red
in a darkroom. A profound kindness
that sees us as good
+ enough. *You are who you choose to be*
said here—late night,
red wine, parked car, still field.
The air hot, charged, but merciful, + we
choose *yes*. Sex. Divine purpose, potential danger—
to be taken down + put back together.

From Les Bourgeois, We Watch the I-70 Bridge Bombing

Rocheport, Missouri

Sunday, bluish + cold as a stillbirth. We wait for the *boom*
like any firework, + breathe when it's late. Fog on the river,
the bridge half visible. MoDOT won't blow it. You smoke
Camels from the bluff top, the vineyard behind us. Birds,
somewhere, rehearsing. Traffic, going west, an army of red
ants stuck in syrup—the highway closed until God's

kind of reckoning comes + levels old steel, leaves a god-
sized hole in Boone County. An hour or so. Then a boom
of sunlight. The fog—lover in a motel bed, rolling over, red-
eyed. MoDOT fires, first, a warning shot under water, river
rippling a little. The second, for us. We flutter like chickens
before a butcher + join in the countdown, chain-smoking

the numbers *3-2-1*. We cover our ears. Gunpowder, smoke—
whole fucking thing drops. A horse falling backwards. God,
it was fast! 63 years + a 1,000 feet of truss. You say *birds*
+ I see their hurry, shelter-torn. Whatever I'm feeling blooms
+ dry rots on the same branch. The sound, after, runs a river
through us [baptism by force, our hair pulled]. You aren't ready

+, scared, drop a $12 bottle of wine, uncorked—oak, cherry,
+ honeysuckle noting your bare ankles. The clouds of smoke
hang as if on a clothesline. Bridge sinking into the riverbed,
all 6 million pounds. The crowd cheers. Applauds. *Goddamn*
you say, over + over, day-drunk. *Fell just like The Towers. Boom!*
Straight down. You talk conspiracies [*jet fuel, inside job*] + vulture-

circle a tragedy, dined on enough. Others hear your birdsong,
your Moscato sermon, + nod. That funny feeling again—red-
hot. Smothering. Am I mortified? Or mourning? I boomerang
around the bluff top + the winery to rid it. Like BBQ smoke
in the eyes, that name—*Les Bourgeois*. "Middle class" in a god-
forsaken farming state. *Booze-wah* you'd laugh, passing Riverboat

Reds in the liquor aisle at Walmart. +, for a while, I did too. *River's
low* you say now, beside me. Here + not. Like the shadow of a hawk
over a hayfield but not the hawk. *How was that bomb?!* It was godly,
I guess. Meaning ferocious + unforgiving. Old Testament. Blood-
obsessed. What if I fear + love it? Love the demolition, air smoky
where the bridge split, + fear that I love *this*. Fear you—booming,

shit-faced—won't get better. On the river, boats + sand barges idle, the red
cranes slow to carry off ruin. The birds will feast on dead fish. *Holy smokes!*
a boy shouts up at his mother, his god, + recreates the scene. *3-2-1—boom!*

ALL SEASONS LANDSCAPING

Jefferson City, Missouri

I am sorry to shovel
city compost with my father
as I am.

        Pitchfork to pile
        to pickup,
        I am more

assured in the harm
    than in the haul—
how surprising + simple the shiv is

           + yet the deadweight, the work, the retrieval,
           makes me a clown,
           child.

My father says nothing.
I'm wearing my good shoes.
I'm weary of the men

in baseball caps + cutoff tees
        who javelin branches
        for the slash, later the shredder—

    they're far too handsome
    + conscious of
    what they're capable of.

        I say nothing
        about this. Only:
        I want to be cremated. Not buried.

The fertilizer has a filth
like sink-sludge, a set of lungs
that exhales *haaaa*

        hot on my forearm.
        My father doesn't say
        Alright, or *Nobody's*

gonna dig up your body,
but sighs this sigh
that begs silence.

        We shovel until
        the truck bed rides low,
        almost scraping. Takes forever

for we must stop
+ pick off what's skewered
from the muck.

        Sticks. Gray grocery
        bags. A Coke can.
        Newspaper.

A scratch off.
Packets of honey
+ soy sauce. A ravel

        of wire. The nipple
        of a baby bottle, aged
        to amber.

        I tell him I'm queer.

Tell Me, Kitty Pryde

What's it like? To escape?
To phase through walls
in smokin' black + gold
but not splatter yourself small?

                    I've tried to ghost. Sucked down
              a pearl necklace of pills, but bricks
         are hard [like knuckles] + that hardness
                  says I'm nothing special.

Do you leave your body behind?
The theatre curtain of blood,
the honeycomb of bones—
where does it go when you're halfway?

                  I'm sure I left mine, somewhere,
             without a leash. It's easier: to get high
       + forget what I'm holding on to. Better if I float
              over him + leave the body to howl.

Or does the world fold around you,
like water when one drops a rock
to wreck its still face? The world—
does it scar first then heal perfect, if at all?

            I can't displace the house or him inside it:
           both are bombproof, + I'm nothing special.
     I always see the hero swoop to save the ingénue—
        but please, Miss Pryde. This time rescue the boy.

New World Recycling

Jefferson City, Missouri

Thrown up + out   of a rust-chewed truck
          + told to be useful—   *grab the bags fuck-*
                              face—
          'cause this garage is greenhouse-hot
+ you, *poor* you,   sweat ropes down your jailbird-arms
          [down a neck you let me kiss   only sometimes].

C'mon fag you laugh   + I stumble into the bed
          for our bales of beer cans,
                    you slapping my ass
                              as I pour
my way across the sticky floor
                    for the conveyor [that great guzzler]
          + empty our empties   into an aluminum rush—
                              the rasp + roil of a wedding car.

          You make sure to feel up

the wet + warm plastic   to pull off cans still stuck
          with a soup-slurp. We drink
                    the sight of our collection
                              wilding up + over, fed
into some basket
          to be weighed. I smile   [my mouth full of silver
                                        + salvage]
          when you read *pounds, pounds,*
                              pounds,
          [more money
                    for more cases]

+ the machine drools   Stag-gold into a blackout   pit,

                    where cans are crushed
                              + cubed.

Harvest

I. Oyster

You cut the mushroom head   + leave it overnight   face down

then a spore print on tinfoil—
       a soft firework   a white fern—

you show me how   to scrape the murmur   with a pocketknife

to score the little life
     into a mason jar   with ryegrass

you can be patient
       easy with me

II. Button

It burned florescent
in the bathroom along the carpet   + bathtub border—

we washed the outside off   only for the mushroom
     to invade

       when you yanked the inch-high stem
as if it were a teenager's   boombox cord
    I unzipped   split down the middle

part of me thanked you
       your willingness
+ the other part
     had lost a comfort—
to no longer see the umbrella
possibly keeping   an unseeable being   dry
       after our shower

III. Trumpet

Once after sex

        we laughed about being fruiting bodies   in Missouri

your breath a warm whistle   across the bottle-mouth of my collarbone

            you said we should flush

                      throughout this season

      before we were found   + picked clean

            but didn't you know

we   were boundless, always   always each other's mushrooms

                  you were my comb tooth

                    + I was your trumpet

IV. Honey Fungus

      Their mycelium reaches for miles

sleeps across state lines

    you tell me   [while we hunt   in early June for coral]

      that if I'm lost among the trees

          don't look for the sun

            but the fungi

        Press your ear to the ground

           Listen for its pulse

              Let the orchard orient you

    I ask   if I were lost

     where would you be

V. Golden Teacher

A generous pinch of psilocybin

brought me to worship

I was a dancer   in wool socks

the world met me   in that

swirl

the bite + thrill

of a tongue kissing a battery

[something like that]

I adored

every layer

of clothing you took off me

until I realized

your hands

were my hands

slowly defeathering

myself

+ you were nowhere

to be found

VI. Shiitake

From an oak older than I'll ever be

to the kitchen stove

stir-fry

shiitakes take

on taste   you tell me

a shadow of other   ingredients

but it's only texture   tough

works the jaw like jerky

smells of a sore   one looks at after   ripping off a band-aid

when you turn away   I spit

VII. Poison Cup

A bouquet of night   tossed down
        the log no longer a dead elm   but a flute of fungi

again + again I asked you   why they were poisonous

no reason you said
        some are just born bad

VIII. Morel

In a magazine   I'm posing
shirtless   a dried-apricot complexion   my nipples pepperoni-pink
I'm wearing morels as fingernails   my mouth giving its best *grrr*
there I'm severe   or sassy stoked   or scared   I can't tell anymore
the title reads MONSTER MORELS
reads MONSTER

it's your favorite picture

GRANDPA'S ICE CREAM + PIES

Lake of the Ozarks, Missouri

A mother on meth. Her boys
    [all skin + ribs + restless] rattle
        a kiddie carousel chained out front.

It's been raining, + the coin-broken horse
    [still + off-white as a fridge] won't budge
        for nothing. The boys no longer cowboys

call out for their mother. *MA!*
    But she's pacing, puppet-like. No shoes.
        With one hand, she rakes her hay-yellow hair,

+ in the other holds
    a pair of purple sunglasses.
        I take my time with my vanilla cone,

watch out the window. A scene
    I've seen + have been actor. Exiting
        the pretty pastel mom-+-pop,

the mother asks for a dollar—
    to buy her boys that chocolate
        key lime pie. Her boys stop to look

over, sticks in high, shaking
    fists—ready to beat the horse
        for being there. Their mother, face picked

burgundy, blue eyes somewhere
     else, mouth just working. I wish I could
         fix her. That fixing her would, in turn,

fix me. Unruin it—
     to be fucked up, + invincible,
            + someone [*God, anyone*] else.

I grab my wallet, about to give her
     all that I have like some fool,
        only to stop at the sound of wood. Snapping.

My Mother Says Lifestyle Instead of Love

One night, a while ago, a wire brush of lightning
      scraped clean the cell tower up the ridge
                          + our landline rang
                              as my room greened like a fish tank.
                  Rang
                    once, twice,
                        then died   in the dark.

2am, my mother calls,
                  + it's *that* disorienting.
          I answer
              + rub my eyes, their whites already printing
                    the headline—
                [*Dad was polishing the rifle . . .*
                        Dad had the tractor
      + brushhog on a hill . . . Dad opened the hive but
      forgot the smoke . . .]

She's Gene Wilder Willy Wonka.   *Did you see this, this Sam Smith Satanist at the*
    Grammys?!

A beer can, in the background.   *People in robes,*
                      performing, I don't know, a ritual!
                        All around fire!
            Which is different,
         I guess, than her church,
                    with pastors in robes
                    performing the Eucharist
        around candlelight.

I'm too tired to say this. I've already woken up my boyfriend. I want to go back to bed.

        Next, she's on about the *LGBEQUZ*
            + again, *again,*
                    my mother says *lifestyle* instead of *love.*

Who are you talking to? from my boyfriend.   From my mother,
                  Who are you talking to?

ALONE

You, Me, Frank Hayes, Sweet Kiss

My favorite record: in 1923, a dead man won a steeplechase. Which was his first race.

I come out to my parents + you break up with me in a text.

The stable hand turned stand-in jockey was Frank Hayes. The horse, a seven-year-old mare, was named Sweet Kiss. + it was her first race.

Your text: *I'm sorry you're feeling this kind of loneliness. I also want to let you know that lately I've been feeling a little emotionally unavailable/detached from the world—*

During the race, Hayes [either 22 or 35, according to some newspapers] suffered a heart attack.

Your text: *You've been so good to me, + I've done my best to reciprocate—but despite that, I don't feel the romantic "spark."*

He slumped over, but remained in the saddle. Sweet Kiss kept on running + crossed the finish line.

The odds: 20-1.

Your text: *I know we talked some before I left, but did we really talk about what we wanted from each other?*

At the finish line, it's said a small crowd ran out to congratulate the two.

Hayes, then, against the horse's neck, fell.

Before you left, I stayed with you + helped you pack. Helped you throw this + that out in the alleyway dumpster.

While some say Frank's heart failed from excitement, others believe it was a result of
having to lose ten pounds in 24 hours, reducing his weight to 130 pounds.

I bought groceries that week. What you didn't pitch, you put back in my hands.

I ate grapes, pickles. Poptarts, granola bars, potato chips, + those yogurt popsicles
you asked for on my car ride home.

Ate until I made myself vomit.

I no longer had a home, then.

Your text: *I didn't really know how I felt [regarding the spark being gone for me]
until you were helping me move, + then I didn't know how to communicate that
to you.*

Out of respect for Hayes, Belmont's jockey club still declared him the winner.

Three days later, he was buried in the same riding silks.

Sometimes, I wear the briefs you mailed me. They're blue + too small.

We haven't spoken since September.

During the race, as Hayes cleared the final jump + passed the winning posts, spectators
took his leaning for love, believed he'd been whispering in the mare's ear.

My second favorite record: being buried alive was so common in the 19th century,
doctors would tie a string to a person's finger, + if that person were to wake up +
move, the string would ring a bell outside the coffin.

Before you left, you kissed me goodbye outside a coffee shop.

Sweet Kiss, after June 4th, never found another rider due to superstition. Retired
after one race.

Tell me, bub: which one of us is the horse + which one the jockey?

For us, should the jockey be called *honesty*?

Is the horse named *heartache*?

The other night, I heard a bell in the dark.

Wanted it to be you. Wanted it to be my mother.

After June 4th, Sweet Kiss was known as *Sweet Kiss of Death*.

Tell me, bub: is our horse fed peppermint + led out to pasture?

Is our horse on a carousel, meant to run a race that never ceases?

Only circles.

You, Me, Disco Baphomet, Broken Thorn Sweet Blackberry

The statue | half-man half-goat | devil | in Iowa's Capitol | in a red robe | goat head a hundred | broken mirrors | + the man | later on TV | said *no one* | *was around* | simply | pulled off the head | with his bare hands | the head being | fabric | glue | being bedazzled | the goat shimmered | in death | the candles | the wreath of flowers | the worship | more vigil now | + I | worshipped you | the half-man half-goat | tattoo | on your arm | a faun | dancing with a Walkman | I remember you | on my chest | as I gave you head | that you called us | *faggots* | affectionately | time to time | + laughed | your devilish laugh | the time you asked | if I'd walk | your beloved beast | a basset hound | only for the dumb dog | to eat dogshit | off the sidewalk | + I | reached in its mouth | struggled to | about pulled off | the dog's head | before it could swallow | was bitten | in the process | thought | *this* | *is love* | a handful | of shit + blood | out of a dog's mouth | only for a text | in the end | you said *it* | *was just casual* | while I | a hundred mirrors | broken | said nothing | looked to the trees | shimmering | the goat | was a girl's | beloved beast | a beautiful thing | she'd brush + bring milk + walk | beside the railroad tracks | the goat | soon stolen | at night | + the boys said *it* | *was a joke* | *nothing* | *but a joke* | but it was | hard work | their little hatchets | the goat screaming | like a half-man | half-devil | the night | dark as a dog's mouth | a death | shimmering | + later the heart | missing | the head | the home | the girl | began to sing | O Disco | Baphomet | Broken Thorn Sweet | Blackberry | my dumb | singing heart | boys | men | are worse devils | will slaughter | something beautiful | bedazzled | beloved | with their bare hands | their little hatchets | boys | being boys | 'cause *no* | *one was around* | *was a joke* | *was nothing* | *was casual* | but I remember the night | I simply pulled off | your shirt | hands above your head | your shorts | your briefs | in the backyard | 'cause it was more | was worship | O | you were a Baphomet | a golden calf | a beautiful thing |

Getting Lost Is What I'm Good At

(w)   Bored, I trouble over cobwebs, cardboard. Mouse poison,   (w)
loose tongues of insulation, + a river-cold black [the flash-
light in my mouth won't stop sheathing its sword] until I
have it again, the Lite-Brite®. My childhood hallelujah.

                                    Then
+ there, I hunt for an outlet. Plug in the box of other light
+ peg the holey paper with whatever bulbs [small bullets]
are left.   The sailboat becomes a volcano, 'cause there's
more orange than blue or green,   + the snowman is a
scarecrow without any white, only yellow.

                             Like what's seen
behind closed eyelids. The blur + blotch. The back of your
head a windmill on fire. A needle into a lean arm. A pipe.
Lightbulb. + I hate what I've done. That I throw the toy
across the attic to hear   it crack. The scatter of pegs the

(w)   sound of tin-roof rain.   (w)

+ the Neurotypical Poet Wrote
Lackofempathy could be a fern

+ by God
I wish it was—
my struggle
only something
of the woods,
viridian + vascular,
finicky about sun
+ shade, birth
+ rebirth
a shot of spores—
what I'm ashamed of
just a fountain of
fronds, their fanning
+ forward flow
as serene +
salubrious as rest.
I would like that.

Rituals

A wish-
bone
is only
wanted
+ worked
to wreck
in two
by two
hands
wishing upon
that wreck.
That's how
it works—
whichever hand
wrecks the largest
bit of bone
wins
the right to wish.
A wish-
ing well
is a hole
in the pocket
of dirt's
dirty overcoat,
our cheap coins
dropped there
believed
to be holy
offerings.
Our worth
worthy
enough for earth

to hear
our beliefs
+ wishes—
our whole
sad story.
A wish-
ful thought
of mine:
the wish-
bone
remains in the bird
unbroken,
+ the wish-
ing well
fills in
+ is pocketless—
broke
in this way.
I wish
you kept me, bub.
Your hands
busy with me.
Wanting.
Maybe I
didn't offer
or break
enough.

Maturing

I handshake branches:
a ruffle of wings, + wild

plums plunge to my feet. I pick
sweet fruit the pink-purple-blue

of a bruise, + t-shirt full,
I come home

to make wine
[+ remember you].

I leave the skins dirty
for their yeast + squeeze

them in both palms,
tempted to drink. To lick

my wounds, myself clean.
I pluck their pits

—they're poisonous—
then add gallons

of well water. Melt an iceberg
of sugar. Let the juices

ferment for two, three
weeks. Maybe this will taste

good—won't be too acidic
or weak. But I won't know

[hadn't known] until
the end. I'll siphon

wine from the carboy
[like I did you, boy,

in your car, your
hand in my hair,

dried wildflowers
on your dashboard]

+ spit, catch the rest
in clear glass bottles.

[We make nothing
that lasts.]

Don't Forget

that while you stress + sweat
over deadlines + your writing,
your overbite + poor eyesight,
the Toyota + its upkeep,
the way others look at you + you
wonder if it's pity or irritation,
revulsion or raw-sugar love, the

                       bees

                              are doing just fine—
                              the workers forage the field to

                       bejewel

their black socks in clover
pollen, + the queen

                       bedazzles

                              other drones back
                              home to the

                       beehive

after her maiden flight
+

                       beguiling

                              flush of pheromones—from there,
                              spring through autumn, the

                       bees

in their white box pulse
*louder than sirens, louder
than bells*, a

                       behemoth

                              of bodies + wings + mouths
                              grooming the queen,
                              saliva-sewing curtains of

                       bee-comb,

their kind

becoming

more of a

bewildering

number, for that is their
nature, their

behavior,

+ all of it was done
without a single thought
or care of you.

Body of a Sister Named Wilhelmina

Gower, Missouri

My body was my own. Now a miracle.
Buried for nearly five years, I'm dug up
By hand, by the hands of my Sisters,
+ show no skeleton, almost no decay—
Only dirt + the white clover of mold
Touch me from when my wood coffin
Caved in. What sunlight + *hallelujahs* met me!

I don't remember how I died. Was it gentle?
Was I in evening prayer, the moon a river
Rising in my room until, swallowed in shine,
I separated? I'm not troubled by this—
I hear the church bells, the *careful careful*
As I'm lifted above my grave. Nothingness
For years, + now the air again, gracing me.

Brought to the chapel, I'm cleaned.
There's talk of a shrine to Saint Joseph,
The patron saint of a Happy Death, + yet
My death marvels! Even my habit, rosary,
+ crucifix are intact! The Sisters prepare
A table with red silk, place a down pillow
For my head. For my face, a mask of candle wax.

I'm back home! O Benedictines of Mary, Queen
Of Apostles—were you Heaven this whole time?
Your humble altar, the cream cloth tinged pink
[A row of peonies] from a spilled Eucharist.
Your tabernacle + Romanesque nave, dizzy
With stained-glass light. But where are the angels,
Their wings + hundreds of eyes? Their Eden-voices?

The Sisters watch over me. They recite psalms
+ rub perfume on my withered hands—not
Having been embalmed, my flesh is as creased +
Worked as newspaper. I want to sit up. Rest
My forehead against theirs—in thanks, in awe, in
Melancholy. Mostly, I want to walk the grounds
+ feel the forthcoming rain. *Please, Sisters*—

A private email has gone public—I'm a sign!
Possibly *incorruptible*. Soon, hundreds of people
Make the pilgrimage: families, the Diocese
Of Kansas City, nonbelievers, NBC News.
They wait behind the door. Inside, my Sisters
Act as if they're building the Ark in a storm,
The flood coming up through the floorboards.

The people form a line, then kneel before
My body. My mouth, still, stitched shut.
I'm gifted rosaries, ox-eye daisies from anxious
Children. Strangers say my name like a hymn +
Pray over me. A few women weep—all touching
My hands, my face. There are cameras + interviews.
Some take, in jars, the grave dirt. I am their God.

O Iron Giant: Denouement

Pick up our junkyard
[our junk-drawer havoc]
tinseled over this town.
Hydraulic hands
in bathroom stalls,
compactor jaw
loose in a baseball dugout.
Crawl back together.
C'mon! We're embarrassing.
Exhausting. How we shred
+ swallow every scrap
of metal tossed our way,
never full. Our halogen lights
can beam so red, the anger
in our haywire-head
large as war. Calm down.
Breathe. We are not
the gun. Only gun-hungry
for some autumn—
hidden away with him.
The woods, railyard, lake water,
a Zale's-spread of stars
before the town woke up
+ his question,
Where did you come from?
We can't have him back
like this. But wasn't it
worth it? Wasn't it
glorious? To love. Trust—
if only for an exhilarating
second. To kamikaze
into a missile + become
a kind of Superman.

Dissection, or To Orphan

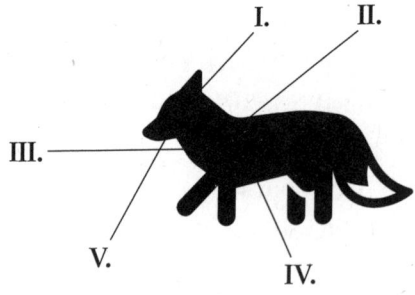

I.

Kit killed   altared on stone   tucked tail to muzzle
I jab his wildness   then pallbear him out of cedar-shade   + into sunlight stinging
my mother from afar   fumed + foxed
that I'd forgotten my Christmas coat out here   until May
her animal-surprise *A fox!* fumed darker   a death-hue

II.

The arc   from thought to action
a run   a ransack   a return
out of the truck's toolbox   two buck knives   blue gloves   my pens + plain paper
This will be anatomy!   *Veterinary!*
we're on our knees kneeling over
my mother + father don't   have Busch or Budweiser in their hands
but euphoria   to eviscerate   evaluate
all of which is just as boozy   just as bamboozling

III.

Slaughter our schooling we riven the red
+ white   fur from fox   fox from fox   our hands trick-or-treating
Here, the lungs!   *The stomach!*   spiked to spill juniper berries   + acid
The heart!   oh the heart
I sketch the damp   the dazzle   best I can
hope to fix it   to our fridge

IV.

+ we become those country folks
giddy with gore   organs for throwing   intestines our double dutch
blood to war paint   drying itchy on cheeks   between fingers
still we hold ceremony   bless the kit
as we scatter him   down a ditch   for other paws
mouths   appetites
we say the Lord's Prayer   *Thy will be done*   + all that
how I cry after   not when my father looks up
+ like airplanes   points out vultures   but when we're inside
a week later   watching *The Fox* + *The Hound* on TV
the part where Tod   discovers a shed of pelts
the part   where Widow Tweed drives Tod to the woods
to abandon him—

V.

Tonight I
would welcome you   mother   father
your once captivation in carnage
whether sober or not   I would welcome   hands
tearing at my animal   to better see it
than to be left behind   in the woods
tonight   the keening   a fox
tonight   the keening   your son

Love Locks

May 14th, 2010—[Robert Nichols] overpowered two juvenile authorities
while riding in a car over the northbound bridge out of Jefferson City.
When the car stopped, he jumped out and plunged more than 50 feet into
the Missouri River. . . . He was handcuffed and shackled to the ankles.

September 3rd, 2019—The body of Lloyd Randall was found Monday
afternoon. . . . The report stated a 2007 Dodge Caliber drove into the
Missouri River Friday night.

—KRCG 13

Up on the pedestrian path,
a riot + ricochet of evening
rain in all that needlework

[arches, trusses, steeple-tall steel],
I run my hands along the locks.
I think of the lives lost.

What they'd say about the railing,
adorned like the Pont des Arts.
About the act itself—

to hook the horseshoe through
the chain link, snap it shut, + pull
out the key [a brass jawbone

held between thumb + index]
only to throw it over + lose
it. Lose it in a river

the color of cardboard—
a river burdened by timber + trash.
All for the metaphor of love. Promise.

+ what would they say to me,
soaked + alone under a streetlight
[a light like holy hell]

as I decorate the mess
of metal with my own lock.
To remember I was loved

once by a man—
but never out-loud, not
here. I don't know. But here,

I'm asking the dead to talk
me off the ledge I hadn't known
I'd be standing on now.

To say *loss is fine*
if it means freedom.
To teach me

to hold + forgive the violences.
Walk in + against the rain, absolutely
alive. To keep the key.

NOTES

"Past + Present Billboards Outside Jefferson City, Missouri" is after Langston Hughes's "Neon Signs" + Aditi Machado's "Billboards." The title is a play on the title of Martin McDonagh's 2017 film *Three Billboards Outside Ebbing, Missouri.* The billboards themselves range from anytime from 2010 until now (2025). The epigraph is taken from the 2007 KRCG 13 article "Millard Case Dismissed."

"Want" is in response to Anders Carlson-Wee's "Pride."

"RollerCoaster Tycoon®" is a coaster + park simulation game by Atari.

The form of "Happy Meal® | Monopoly" is after a pair of McDonald's Monopoly stickers, a sales promotion run by the fast-food restaurant chain.

The form of "Tractor Implements: A Manual" is after A. E. Stallings's "First Love: A Quiz."

"O Iron Giant: [Establishing Shot]," "[Double Exposure]," "[Denouement]," is inspired by + in conversation with Brad Bird's 1999 animated film *The Iron Giant.* Mention[s] of queer intimacy + neurodivergence are the author's own.

"Gorgeous" borrows a line from Ocean Vuong's poem "On Earth We're Briefly Gorgeous" + follows the golden shovel form, after Terrance Hayes.

"XXX" + "Don't Forget" are part of a nonce form by the author, called "Shakes," invented with the help of Carl Phillips. The form is inspired by a personal stim [pacing] + experience with echolalia [involuntary repetition of words, phrases, or sounds from someone else]. The form also includes a song lyric—*heaven is here if you want it* in "XXX" is from Florence + the Machine's "Heaven Is Here," + *louder than sirens, louder than bells* in "Don't Forget" is from Florence + the Machine's "Drumming Song."

The form of "Deer Season, Youth Firearms. You're 13" is after Leila Chatti's "Tumor."

"Headless" includes Microsoft 365 icons as headers.

The epigraph in "What Hunts Us Back" is taken from a 2019 KRCG 13 article "Conservation Agents Uses Cardboard Cutouts to Dispel Rumor of Recent Mountain Lion Sighting."

"*Isobutyl Nitrite*" refers to the recreational drug "poppers" + reflects on Boaz Yakin's 2000 biographical sports film *Remember the Titans*.

The bridge demolition mentioned in "From LES BOURGEOIS, We Watch the I-70 Bridge Bombing" took place on September 10, 2023.

Kitty Pryde, in "Tell Me, Kitty Pryde," is a fictional superhero able to phase through solid matter. She appears in the *X-Men* universe, as well as other Marvel Comics.

"You, Me, Frank Hayes, Sweet Kiss" owes a debt to Pauline Murphy's "Flogging a Dead Jockey | The Bizarre Death of Frank Hayes," published on *Headstuff*, + Bianca Britton's "Frank Hayes: The Jockey Who Won a Race Despite Being Dead," published on CNN.

"You, Me, Disco Baphomet, Broken Thorn Sweet Blackberry" is after Brigit Pegeen Kelly's "Song" + references the December 14, 2023, beheading of the Satanic Temple's Baphomet statue in the Iowa State Capitol building.

A Lite-Brite is a toy invented by Burt Meyer Dalia Verbickas, + Joseph M. Burck + sold by Hasbro. It consists of a light box with small, colored plastic pegs that fit into a panel + illuminate to create a lit picture.

"+ the Neurotypical Poet Wrote *Lackofempathy could be a fern*" is in response to Carolina Ebeid's "Veronicas of a Matador."

"Body of a Sister Named Wilhelmina" is after Thomas James's "Mummy of a Lady Named Jemutesonekh" + inspired by the exhumation of Mary Wilhelmina Lancaster on May 18, 2023, when her body was discovered as possibly "incorrupt."

"Dissection, or To Orphan" includes Microsoft 365 icon + references Ted Berman, Richard Rich, + Art Stevens's 1981 animated film *The Fox and the Hound*. The poem's ending pays tribute to Elijah Burrell's "Reverberations."

The epigraphs in "Love Locks" are from a 2011 KRCG 13 article "One Year Later: DSS Won't Say How Teen Escaped and Jumped Off Missouri River Bridge" + a 2019 KRCG 13 article "Highway Patrol Identifies 18-Year-Old Found in Missouri River as Jefferson City Teen," respectively.

ACKNOWLEDGMENTS

Awe + adoration to Brenda Hillman. Your writing grabs + guides my own, + I'm so grateful for your belief in this book + for such a beautiful foreword.

Deep gratitude to Nicole-Anne Keyton, my incredible + incredibly kind editor. Your dedication + care catapulted the book to its best.

To the terrific team at Beacon Press, Beth Dial, + the National Poetry Series—I can't thank you enough for this honor.

Many thanks to the editors + readers of the following journals, where these poems first appeared or are forthcoming, sometimes in different forms + titles:

Afternoon Visitor: "Getting Lost Is What I'm Good At"
Bear Review: "What Hunts Us Back"
Bennington Review: "ALL SEASONS LANDSCAPING," "O Iron Giant: Double Exposure"
Berkeley Poetry Review: "Hillbilly Swimming Pool"
Blood Orange Review: "Headless"
Cider Press Review: "Gorgeous," "Tell Me, Kitty Pryde"
Denver Quarterly: "Body of a Sister Named Wilhelmina"
GASHER: "Maturing"
Gulf Coast: "Always," "Want"
Hayden's Ferry Review: "XXX"
Heavy Feather Review: "Halloween"
Iron Horse Literary Review: "Dissection, or To Orphan"
Longleaf Review: "Rituals"
The Missouri Review: "Love Locks," "Wash"

Moon City Review: "Border Collie"

Nashville Review: "You, Me, Disco Baphomet, Broken Thorn Sweet Blackberry"

Nat. Brut: "O Iron Giant: Establishing Shot"

Neon Door: "NEW WORLD RECYCLING"

The New Territory: "Deer Season, Youth Firearms. You're 13"

Oxford American: "My Mother Says *Lifestyle* Instead of *Love*"

Pleaides: "Harvest"

Poetry Online: "Any Fire"

Puerto del Sol: "FEARFEST"

Quarterly West: "Don't Forget," "Special K"

Shankpainter: "Cauldron"

Small Orange: "Hometown"

Sugar House Review: "RollerCoaster Tycoon® + the Tyrant I Was"

Swamp Ape Review: "Black Cat," "Tractor Implements: A Manual"

Third Coast: "From LES BOURGEOIS, We Watch the I-70 Bridge Bombing,"
    "GRANDPA'S ICE CREAM + PIES," "O Iron Giant: Denouement"

Waxwing: "Remains"

"You, Me, Frank Hayes, Sweet Kiss" appeared in *Best New Poets 2022*, selected by Paula Bohince.

An earlier version of "Love Locks" was selected for *The Missouri Review* 2022 Poem of the Year.

Many of the poems first appeared in the chapbook *LOVE LOCKS*, which was selected for *Quarterly West*'s 2022 Chapbook Contest. Endless gratitude to Luther Hughes, Audrey Bauman, Garrett Biggs, Jessica Tanck, + the *Quarterly West* team!

I'm grateful for the following institutions + residencies for the support + space to write *OHHV*: Lincoln University of Missouri, Washington University in St. Louis, University of Utah, the Fine Arts Work Center in Provincetown, Monson Arts, + Vermont Studio Center.

OHHV would not exist without the wisdom, guidance, grace, + encouragement of my professors. My heart goes out to Mary Jo Bang, Elijah Burrell, Mark Bibbins, Tina Casagrand Foss, Katharine Coles, Eduardo C. Corral, Daren Dean, Cass Donish, francine j. harris, Niki Herd, Nathan McClain, Edward McPherson, Jacqueline Osherow, Carl Phillips, Roger Reeves, + Paisley Rekdal.

To my friends, all such amazing artists + wonderful souls. I'm blessed to know you + your work—

Bob Boldt, Sarah Davis, Will Edwards, Mason Finch, Cameron Forrest, Tasia Kohlheim, Dontay Phillips, Terrell Pickens, Jenecia Sims, + Benjamin Zaiger II.

Mary Helen Callier, Maddy Frank, Abbey Frederick, Asha Futterman, Carlota Gamboa, Stefania Gomez, Naomi Gordon-Loebl, Joe Gutierrez, Kathryn Hargett-Hsu, Edil Hassan, Joseph Gunho Jang, mace dent johnson, Dighan Kelly, Safa Khatib, Sydney Kilcoyne, Nora Kipnis, Caleb Lewis, Cora Lewis, Asjylyn Loder, Precious Musa, Kelan Nee, Angel Adaeze Ogoemesim, Sanam Sheriff, Seth Wang, + Pritha RaySircar.

Laura Cresté, Blake Daniels, Emsaki, Mark Joshua Epstein, Willie Fitzgerald, Elizabeth Flood, Kim Coleman Foote, Yahna Harris, Jinee Siennie Lee, John Murillo, Hannah Perrin King, Pieter Paul Pothoven, Christa Romanosky, Tinja Ruusuvuori, Clarisse Baleja Saïdi, Sarah Stern, Jorrell Watkins, + Sichong Xie.

Gabe Brown, Shaina Gates, Tavi Gevinson, Elijah Hamilton-Wray, Kristin Kearns, + Erin Malone.

Janan Alexandra, Sheryl Anaya, Sarah Audsley, Dimelza Broche, Julia Cannon, Elendë Connor, Serra Fels, Bianca Fields, Andrew Harrison, Rose Howse, Emad Jabini, Adrienne Kinsella, Mary Larsen, Casandra Lopez, Claire Luchette, Malia Maxwell, Meredith Moore, Sarah Sagarin, Kira Saks, Jeneé Skinner, Lydia Smith, Jasmine Tabor, Mirabel Wigon, Jamele Wright, Jiawei Zhao, + Luba Zygarewicz.

Mohammad Afaan, Allie Field Bell, Sunny Carlstrom, Jessica Challis, Stephanie Choi, Alexandra Duringer, Sophie Gauthier, Matty Layne Glasgow, Chengru He, Jannah Hinthorne, Kasimma, Jasmine Khaliq, Saxton Nelson, Erin O'Luanaigh, Blair Reilly, Vitasta Singh, Jamie L. Smith, Matthew Tuckner, Erick Verran, Weiji Wang, + Lindsey Webb.

To my soulmates, my kindreds: Georgia Dickie, Stefania Gomez, Kristy Hughes, + Gothataone Moeng. When I think + write of light, you're there.

What I know of poetry, of storytelling, + of love comes from my family. Bhion Achimba. Missouri. Thank you for holding me + saving my life. I'll carry you, always.